Homework Helpers
Reading Grade 1

As a parent, you want your child to enjoy learning and to do well in school. The activities in the *Homework Helpers* series will help your child develop the skills and self-confidence that lead to success. Humorous illustrations and diverse formats make the activities interesting for your child.

HOW TO USE THIS BOOK

- Provide a quiet, comfortable place to work with your child.

- Plan a special time to work with your child. Create a warm, accepting atmosphere so your child will enjoy spending this time with you. Limit each session to one or two activities.

- Make sure your child understands the directions before beginning an activity.

- Check the answers with your child as soon as an activity has been completed. (Be sure to remove the answer pages from the center of the book before your child uses the book.)

- The activities in this book were selected from previously published Frank Schaffer materials.

- Topics covered in this book are color and number words, sight words, opposite words, classification, following directions, and comprehension skills such as finding facts, drawing conclusions, and making inferences.

ISBN #0-86734-103-3

FS-8136 Homework Helpers—Reading Grade 1
All rights reserved—Printed in the U.S.A.
Copyright © 1991 Frank Schaffer Publications, Inc.
23740 Hawthorne Blvd., Torrance, CA 90505

This Book Belongs To

Name _____

Date _____

Draw the correct number of pictures. Color correctly.

1. Draw two red 🧤's.	
2. Draw four green 🧦's.	3. Draw one yellow 🧢.
4. Draw five blue 👜's.	5. Draw three purple 👝's.
6. Draw seven black 🎩's.	7. Draw nine orange 🧦's.

☐ Color five 's yellow. Color one blue.

☐ Color nine 's black. Color three orange.

☐ Color seven 's red. Color five brown.

☐ Color six 's yellow. Color eight blue.

☐ Color four 's purple. Color two green.

Circle the correct word for each picture.
Color the pictures.

1. blue / cat / cow	**2.** sun / leg / snake	**3.** bed / horse / boat
4. goat / feet / girl	**5.** frog / bike / fish	**6.** dog / duck / puppy
7. book / baby / moon	**8.** gate / lamb / gas	**9.** boy / bone / coat
10. rabbit / egg / eye	**11.** snake / skate / monkey	**12.** house / light / horse

Draw a line from **each** picture to the correct word.
Color the pictures.

 1.

ladder

cake

7.

2.

airplane

fox

8.

3.

bike

duck

9.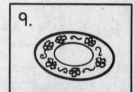

4.

ball

kitten

10.

5.

car

dish

11.

6.

dress

truck

12.

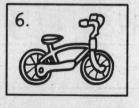

A Lost Dog

Gus had a dog named Jake.
His big black and white dog is lost.

1. What did Gus have?

_____

_____

2. What color is Jake?

_____

_____

3. Was Jake big or little?

_____

_____

4. Where is Jake?

_____

_____

5. Do you think Gus is happy or sad?

_____

_____

Write the opposite of each word on the line.

walk   girl
out   work
dry   push

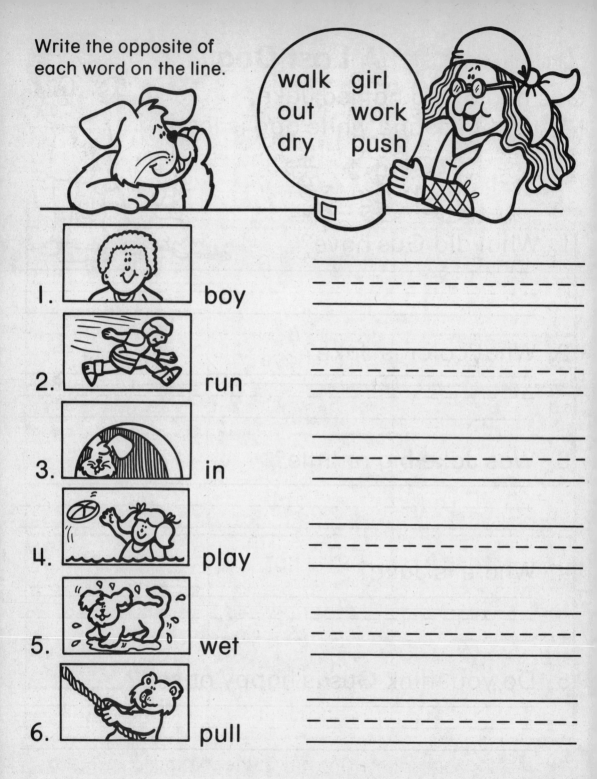

1. boy _____

2. run _____

3. in _____

4. play _____

5. wet _____

6. pull _____

Circle the two words that make each contraction.

1.	he's	he is	he will
2.	I'm	I have	I am
3.	we've	we have	we will
4.	isn't	is not	has not
5.	she'll	she will	she is
6.	they're	we are	they are
7.	wasn't	are not	was not
8.	let's	let us	they are
9.	here's	she is	here is
10.	that'll	that will	he will

*Write three sentences, using any of the contractions above.

Blaze

Liz rode on Blaze.
She put her hand on his mane.

1. Do you think Blaze is a dog?

2. Why do you think that?

3. Who rode on Blaze?

4. Did you ever see a horse?

5. Do you have a mane?

At the Farm

Write the sentences.
Use the words that match the pictures.

The  milks the  .

The  has a  .

The  is in the  .

Pet Hunt

Circle the words.
The words go → and ↓.

| fish |
| dog |
| bird |
| pony |

```
f  p  o  n  y
i  a  p  s  r
s  k  d  o  g
h  b  i  r  d
```

Write the word in the sentence.

1. My _____ has fins.

2. A _____ can fly.

3. I ride my _____.

4. The _____ barks.

A Busy Day

Write the sentences.
Use the words that match the pictures.

teacher   plant   book   boy   girl   desk

The waters a .

_____

_____

The reads a .

_____

_____

A has a .

_____

_____

Pets

Don has six pet fish in a tank.
Don has a fat yellow cat, too.

1. Where are the fish?

   _____

   _____

2. How many fish does Don have?

   _____

   _____

3. What does Don's cat look like?

   _____

   _____

4. Do you have a pet?

   _____

   _____

5. Do you think the cat will eat the fish?

   _____

   _____

Plant Parts We Eat

Read each riddle. Write the answer.

carrot   pumpkin   lettuce   celery   corn

1. I am big and round.
   I am an orange fruit.
   Make me into pie.

   _____

   - - - - - - - - - - - - - - - - - -

2. I am yellow.
   I am a seed.
   Put butter on me.

   _____

   - - - - - - - - - - - - - - - -

   _____

3. I am orange.
   I am a root.
   Rabbits like me.

   _____

   - - - - - - - - - - - - - -

   _____

4. I am a leaf.
   I am green.
   Put me in salad.

   _____

   - - - - - - - - - - - - - - - -

   _____

5. I am a crunchy
   stem. Try me with
   peanut butter.

   _____

   - - - - - - - - - - - - - -

   _____

Is It a Bird?

Birds have feathers.
Most birds can fly.
Some birds eat seeds.

1. What do birds have?

_ _

2. What can most birds do?

_ _

3. What do some birds eat?

_ _

Draw two birds. Color the picture.

Neighborhood Helpers

Write the name of the correct helper.

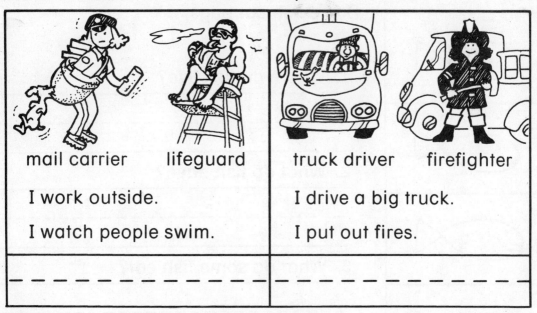

mail carrier   lifeguard

I work outside.

I watch people swim.

_ _ _ _ _ _ _ _ _ _ _ _

truck driver   firefighter

I drive a big truck.

I put out fires.

_ _ _ _ _ _ _ _ _ _ _ _

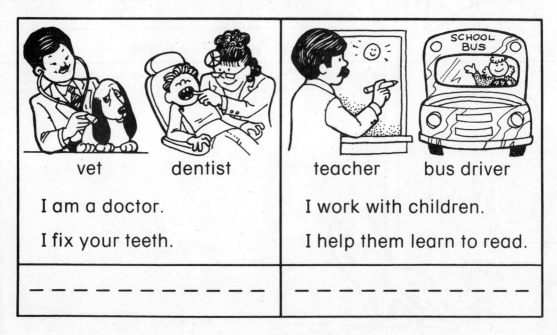

vet   dentist

I am a doctor.

I fix your teeth.

_ _ _ _ _ _ _ _ _ _ _ _

teacher   bus driver

I work with children.

I help them learn to read.

_ _ _ _ _ _ _ _ _ _ _ _

In the Pond

Fish live in water.
Fish have scales.
Some fish eat bugs.

1. Where do fish live?

   _____

   - - - - - - - - - - - - - - - - - -

   _____

2. What do fish have?

   _____

   - - - - - - - - - - - - - - - - - -

   _____

3. What do some fish eat?

   _____

   - - - - - - - - - - - - - - - - - -

   _____

Draw some fish in the water.

Wally Walrus

This walrus is fat.
Fat keeps him warm.
He swims in cold water.

1. What is Wally? _____

   _____

2. Where does Wally swim? _____

   _____

3. What does fat do for Wally? _____

   _____

Draw a walrus on the ice.

Pete

Pete can fly up in the sky.
Pete has a big orange beak.

There he goes !

1. Is Pete a little boy?
   _____
   -
   _____

2. How do you know that?
   _____
   -
   _____

3. Where does Pete fly?
   _____
   -
   _____

4. What color is his beak?
   _____
   -
   _____

5. Can you fly?
   _____
   -
   _____

Circle three pictures in each row that go together.

1.

2.

3.

4.

5.

6.

*Color the pictures.

FS-8136 Homework Helpers—Reading 1

Name That Tiger

Write the word from the Word Box that tells about the list of words on each tiger.

Word Box

space farm
tools insects
food dishes

barn
horse
cow

1. _____

bowl
plate
cup

2. _____

drill
hammer
saw

3. _____

sun
moon
stars

4. _____

bee
ladybug
butterfly

5. _____

apple
milk
cheese

6. _____

Brainwork! Add one more word to the list on each tiger.

Rainbowsaurus

Color the spots with toy words yellow.
Color the spots with clothing words red.
Color the spots with animal words blue.

kite
doll
hen
fish
coat
dress
ball
hat
bike
dog
cat
pants
pig

Brainwork! Make a list of 10 things in your bedroom closet.

21

Group It

Fill in the circles next to words
that belong in each group.

1. **Colors**

   - ○ red
   - ○ blue
   - ○ truck
   - ○ green
   - ○ cat
   - ○ yellow

2. **Food**

   - ○ bat
   - ○ milk
   - ○ egg
   - ○ meat
   - ○ dress
   - ○ apple

3. **People**
   - ○ tree
   - ○ girl
   - ○ mother
   - ○ father
   - ○ boy
   - ○ fox

4. **Numbers**

   - ○ five
   - ○ one
   - ○ frog
   - ○ three
   - ○ four
   - ○ sock

5. **Parts of the Body**

   - ○ ear
   - ○ arm
   - ○ hand
   - ○ head
   - ○ nose
   - ○ shoe

6. **Weather**

   - ○ grass
   - ○ rain
   - ○ cloud
   - ○ fog
   - ○ boot
   - ○ snow

7. **School**

   - ○ book
   - ○ desk
   - ○ sun
   - ○ pencil
   - ○ flag
   - ○ bird

8. **House**

   - ○ lamp
   - ○ bed
   - ○ door
   - ○ sink
   - ○ hat
   - ○ rug

Brainwork! Make a list of baby animal names.

Color animals you find...

...in the desert

...on a farm

...in a circus

red

yellow

blue

FS-8136 Homework Helpers—Reading 1

Animals Care for Their Babies

Read the animal facts.
Circle the names of the animals.

1. The father penguin keeps his baby warm.

2. A cheetah shows her babies how to hunt.

3. The seal helps her baby learn to swim.

4. A monkey cleans its baby.

Write the animal name.

Pull-Out
Answers

Remove these answer pages
before your child uses the book.

Pull-Out Answers

Pages One to Two
self-explanatory

Page Three
1. cat
2. sun
3. boat
4. girl
5. frog
6. duck
7. book
8. gas
9. bone
10. eye
11. skate
12. house

Page Four
1. airplane
2. ball
3. cake
4. truck
5. fox
6. bike
7. car
8. ladder
9. dish
10. dress
11. kitten
12. duck

Page Five
1. a dog named Jake
2. black and white
3. big
4. lost
5. sad

Page Six
1. girl
2. walk
3. out
4. work
5. dry
6. push

Page Seven
1. he is
2. I am
3. we have
4. is not
5. she will
6. they are
7. was not
8. let us
9. here is
10. that will

Page Eight
1. no
2. A dog doesn't have a mane.
3. Liz
4. answer varies
5. no

Page Nine
The boy milks the cow.
The girl has a cat.
The pig is in the mud.

Page Ten
1. fish
2. bird
3. pony
4. dog

Page Eleven
The girl waters a plant.
The boy reads a book.
The teacher has a desk.

Page Twelve
1. in a tank
2. six
3. fat and yellow
4. answer varies
5. answer varies

Page Thirteen
1. pumpkin
2. corn
3. carrot
4. lettuce
5. celery

Page Fourteen
1. feathers
2. fly
3. seeds

Page Fifteen
lifeguard
firefighter
dentist
teacher

Page Sixteen
1. in water
2. scales
3. bugs

Page Seventeen
1. a walrus
2. in cold water
3. keeps him warm

Page Eighteen
1. no
2. A boy can't fly. A boy does not have a beak.
3. in the sky
4. orange
5. no

Page Nineteen
1. stool, couch, bench
2. strawberries, orange, pears
3. starfish, seal, jellyfish
4. dress, woman's hat, high heels
5. basketball, tennis racket, football
6. cow, goat, sheep

Page Twenty
1. farm
2. dishes
3. tools
4. space
5. insects
6. food

Page Twenty-one
Colored yellow—bike, ball, doll, kite

Colored red—hat, pants, dress, coat

Colored blue—cat, dog, hen, fish, pig

Pull-Out Answers

Page Twenty-two
1. red, blue, green, yellow
2. milk, egg, meat, apple
3. girl, mother, father, boy
4. five, one, three, four
5. ear, arm, hand, head, nose
6. rain, cloud, fog, snow
7. book, desk, pencil, flag
8. lamp, bed, door, sink, rug

Page Twenty-three
Colored red—scorpion, lizard, roadrunner, camel
Colored yelllow—cow, duck, pig, chicks
Colored blue—elephant, bear, tiger, lion

Page Twenty-four
1. penguin
2. cheetah
3. seal
4. monkey
seal, monkey, penguin, cheetah

Page Twenty-five
1. dime
2. jump
3. four
4. shoes
5. blue
6. toes
7. month
8. dinner
9. jelly
10. stars

Page Twenty-six
Answers will vary.

Page Twenty-seven
1. no
2. It came to smell Dan.
3. no
4. still
5. answer varies

Page Twenty-eight
self-explanatory

Page Twenty-nine
self-explanatory

Page Thirty
1. desert tortoise
2. cactus
3. brown
4. in a hole

Page Thirty-one
Bunny in the Bushes
Asleep for the Winter

Page Thirty-two
1. No   2. Yes
The dogs are big and little.

1. Yes   2. No
The chick is hatching.

1. No   2. Yes   3. No
She loves her pet.

Page Thirty-three
1. The bobcat hunts mice.
2. The bat can hang upside down.
3. The tree frog can climb.
4. The river otter is playing.
5. The giraffe is taller than the boy.

Page Thirty-four
1. The boy smells the flowers.
2. The bird feeds her babies.
3. It is a windy day.
4. The girl sees the butterfly.
5. The girl waters the flowers.

Page Thirty-five
1. Jill
2. Bill
3. Jill
4. by Bill's blue house
5. answer varies

Page Thirty-six
1. hat
2. man
3. hide
4. rabbit
5. out

Page Thirty-seven
1. a hug
2. Kim, Dad, and I
3. tag
4. answer varies
5. answer varies

Page Thirty-eight
1. yes
2. no
3. no
4. yes
5. yes
6. no
7. no
8. yes
9. no

Page Thirty-nine
1. a
2. c
3. f
4. b
5. d
6. e

Page Forty
1. a
2. b
3. b
4. a
5. b

Page Forty-one
1. a
2. a
3. b
4. a
5. b
6. b

Pull-Out Answers

Page Forty-two
1. Fluff
2. no
3. fish
4. from a can
5. no

Page Forty-three
1. Panda
2. Turtle
3. Moose and Panda
4. 11 months

Page Forty-four
1. no
2. no
3. yes
4. no
It was the best campout.

Page Forty-five
Jean found her lost bear.
Jim got new shoes.
The cat wanted milk, too.

Page Forty-six
Answers will vary but should
be similar to the following:
- Shelby can do tricks.
- Red Fox drove too fast.

Page Forty-seven
1. the sun
2. the wind
3. the man
4. a coat
5. It is hot.

Page Forty-eight
1. fox
2. jumps
3. grapes
4. misses
5. not good
6. many times
7. up high

Three of a Kind

Use the words in the Word Box.
Write another word for each group.

Word Box

jump	stars
four	dime
toes	shoes
month	blue
dinner	jelly

1. penny, nickel, _____

2. hop, skip, _____

3. two, three, _____

4. shirt, pants, _____

5. red, white, _____

6. legs, feet, _____

7. day, week, _____

8. breakfast, lunch, _____

9. peanut butter, bread, _____

10. sun, moon, _____

Brainwork! Write a word that tells about each group of words above. Example: penny, nickel, dime—money.

Make a List

Write names of things that belong in each group.

Things at the Beach

_____
- - - - - - - - - -
_____
- - - - - - - - - -
_____
- - - - - - - - - -
_____

Kinds of Clothes

_____
- - - - - - - - - -
_____
- - - - - - - - - -
_____
- - - - - - - - - -
_____

Animals That Swim

_____
- - - - - - - - - -
_____
- - - - - - - - - -
_____
- - - - - - - - - -
_____

Parts of a Tree

- - - - - - - - - -
_____
- - - - - - - - - -
_____
- - - - - - - - - -
_____

Things in a Salad

- - - - - - - - - -
_____
- - - - - - - - - -
_____
- - - - - - - - - -
_____

Brainwork! Draw pictures of the things in one of the lists above.

The Deer

Dan sat so very still.
A little deer came to smell him.

1. Did Dan run and yell?

_____

_____

2. What did the deer do?

_____

_____

3. Was it a big deer?

_____

_____

4. How did Dan sit?

_____

_____

5. Why do you think Dan did that?

_____

_____

1. Color Ann's ⌒⌒ red.

2. Color Andy's ⌒⌒ orange.

3. Make a yellow ⋈ for Ann.

4. Color Ann's ⋈ blue.

5. Color Ann's 👁 's green.

6. Color Andy's 👁 's brown.

7. Make a red 👄 for Ann.

8. Make Andy's ⊙ s black.

Color the picture.

Follow each direction.

1. Draw a line under the king.

2. Circle the fox.

3. Draw a line from the sun to the wind.

4. Draw a 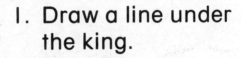 around the mouse.

5. Put a line above the lion.

6. Put an X on the rabbit.

7. Put a fat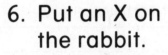 on the turtle.

8. Draw two lines from the turtle to the rabbit.

*Color the pictures.

The Desert Tortoise

Read the story. Write the answers.

Look at the brown desert tortoise.
It moves very slowly.
It eats cactus.
The tortoise digs a hole.
It sleeps in the hole.

1. What moves very slowly?

_____

_____

2. What does the desert tortoise eat?

_____

_____

3. What color is the desert tortoise?

_____

_____

4. Where does it sleep?

_____

_____

Look at the picture.
Circle and write the best title.

Bunny in the Bushes   Bunny Friends
Sleeping Bunny   The Rabbit Nest

_____

- -

_____

Snow in Winter   Brown Mouse
Time to Play   Asleep for the Winter

_____

- -

_____

Brainwork! Write a story about one of the pictures above.

The **main idea** tells about the whole picture.

Does the sentence tell the main idea of the picture?
Fill in **yes** or **no**. Then write the main idea sentence.

	Yes	No
1. The dog plays.	O	O
2. The dogs are big and little.	O	O

_____

- - - - - - - - - - - - - - - - - -

_____

	Yes	No
1. The chick is hatching.	O	O
2. The chick is big.	O	O

_____

- - - - - - - - - - - - - - - - - -

_____

	Yes	No
1. The pet is furry.	O	O
2. She loves her pet.	O	O
3. Her pet is little.	O	O

_____

- - - - - - - - - - - - - - - - - -

_____

Brainwork! Draw pictures of four animals you like.

The **main idea** tells about the whole picture.

Which sentence tells the main idea of the picture?
Fill in the circle next to the correct answer.

1.

○ The bobcat has a tail.
○ The bobcat hunts mice.

2.

○ The bat has wings.
○ The bat can hang upside
   down.

3.

○ The tree frog is green.
○ The tree frog can climb.

4.

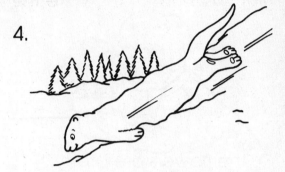

○ The river otter is playing.
○ It is snowing.
○ The river otter has fur.

5.

○ The boy is happy.
○ The giraffe is taller than
   the boy.
○ Giraffes have long necks.

Brainwork! Cut out a picture from an old magazine. Paste it
on writing paper. Write a sentence that tells the main idea.

The **main idea** tells about the whole picture.

Which sentence tells the main idea of the picture?
Fill in the circle next to the correct answer.

1.

○ The flowers are pretty.
○ The boy smells the flowers.

2.

○ The bird feeds her babies.
○ The babies are in the nest.

3.

○ The leaves are falling.
○ It is a windy day.

4.

○ The butterfly is on the tree.
○ The girl sees the butterfly.
○ It is spring.

5.

○ The girl is outside.
○ The plants are growing.
○ The girl waters the flowers.

Brainwork! Find a picture in a book. Copy it on drawing paper. Write a sentence that tells the main idea.

Home Sweet Home

Jill has a big brown house.
Bill has a little blue house by a tree.

1. Who has the big house?

_____

_____

2. Who has the blue house?

_____

_____

3. Who has the brown house?

_____

_____

4. Where is the tree?

_____

_____

5. Do you have a brown house?

_____

_____

Read the story.

The rabbit can hide.
The rabbit hides in the hat.
You can not see the rabbit.
The man looks in the hat.
He takes out the rabbit.
Surprise!

Circle the right answer.

1. The rabbit is in a _____ .   hat   man

2. The _____ looks in the hat.   girl   man

3. The rabbit can _____ .   hide   talk

4. The _____ is in the hat.   man   rabbit

5. The rabbit comes _____ .   down   out

Fun with Dad

Not it!

Dad gave Kim and me a big hug.
Then we went out to play tag with him.

1. What did Dad give me?

_____

_____

2. Who went out to play?

_____

_____

3. What did we play?

_____

_____

4. Can you play tag?

_____

_____

5. Do you like to win when you play?

_____

_____

Think! Is it true?
Circle **yes** or **no**.

1. A dog likes to play.   yes   no

2. A bike can swim.   yes   no

3. A house can run.   yes   no

4. A duck can swim.   yes   no

5. You can wash your hands.   yes   no

6. A baby can fly.   yes   no

7. A fox can ride a bike.   yes   no

8. A frog can jump.   yes   no

9. Bill has four legs.   yes   no

*Where you circled no, change one of the words to make the sentence true.

Write the letter of the correct picture for each riddle.

___ 1. I went in a house.
I saw three bears.
I ran home.
Who am I?

___ 2. I come out at night.
You see me in the sky.
Make a wish!
Who am I?

___ 3. I live in water.
I am a fish.
I am a girl too.
How can that be?

___ 4. I live in a lamp.
I can give you things.
What is your wish?
Who am I?

___ 5. I want to be a boy.
I am made of wood.
I told a lie.
I have a long nose.

___ 6. I sat on a wall.
I fell off.
No one can help me.
Who am I?

How are the two pictures alike?
Circle the right answer.

a. Both are little.

b. Both are girls.

a. Both can run.

b. Both can fly.

a. Both are real.

b. Both live in water.

a. Both can sleep.

b. Both can read.

a. Both can swim.

b. Both can fall.

Circle the sentence that tells what will happen next.

1.

a. You will run fast.
b. You will play with it.

2.

a. He will melt.
b. He will go home.

3.

a. The boy will look at T.V.
b. He will pick up his toys.

4.

a. She will blow out the candles.
b. She will eat the cake.

5.

a. He will ride his bike.
b. He will ride his sled.

6.

a. They will walk to school.
b. They will get on the bus.

My Pet Cat

My cat Fluff will not eat mice.
She likes to eat fish from a can.

1. What is the cat's name?

_____

_____

2. Will my cat eat mice?

_____

_____

3. What does she like to eat?

_____

_____

4. Where does she get the fish?

_____

_____

5. Is the cat a boy cat?

_____

_____

Months With Mom

The chart shows about how long some baby animals live with their mothers.

Coyote	6 months
Owl	1 month
Moose	12 months
Panda	18 months
Turtle	0 months

Fill in the circle next to the correct answer.

1. Which animal stays with its mother the longest?

   ○ turtle   ○ moose   ○ panda   ○ coyote

2. Which animal does not stay with its mother?

   ○ owl   ○ turtle   ○ coyote   ○ moose

3. Which two animals stay longer than the coyote?

   ○ owl and panda   ○ turtle and panda
   ○ moose and panda   ○ moose and owl

4. How much longer does the moose stay with its mother than the owl? (Hint: Subtract the numbers.)

   ○ 9 months   ○ 8 months   ○ 11 months

The **main idea** tells about the whole story.

Read the story.

Mike helped pitch the tent.
Amy cooked a hot dog.
Dad told a funny story.
It was the best campout.

Does the sentence tell the main idea? Write **yes** or **no**.

1. Amy cooked a hot dog.

_____

2. Dad told a funny story.

_____

3. It was the best campout.

_____

4. Mike helped pitch the tent.

_____

Write the sentence that tells the main idea.

_____

Brainwork! List things you need to take on a camping trip.

The **main idea** tells about the whole story.

Read each story.
Circle the sentence below it that tells the main idea.

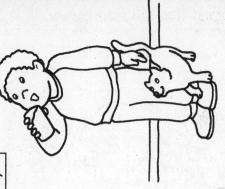

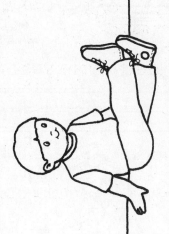

Jean lost her teddy bear.
She looked in the closet.
She checked the shelf.
Then she found the bear
in her toy box. She gave
it a big hug.

Jean hugged the bear.
Jean had a toy box.
Jean found her lost bear.

Jim's sneakers were old.
They had holes in them.
His mom took him to the
shoe store. He got a
new pair of shoes. They
had red and blue
shoelaces.

Mom went shopping.
The shoes had holes.
Jim got new shoes.

Juan was drinking milk.
Suddenly he felt
something furry rub
against his leg. It was his
cat. She wanted some
milk, too. Juan put some
in her dish.

Juan was scared.
The cat wanted milk, too.
Juan's cat was furry.

Brainwork! Write a four-sentence story. Let a friend find the main idea of the story.

 FS-8136 Homework Helpers—Reading 1

The **main idea** tells about the whole story.

Read the story carefully. Look at all the details in the story.
Then write a sentence telling the main idea.

Shelby lives in the woods.
She is a little turtle.
Shelby can do tricks.
This is her best one.
She turns over and spins
on her shell.

_____
- -
_____

Red Fox likes to drive his car.
One day he drove too fast.
A police officer stopped him.
She gave Red Fox a ticket.
That was not fun.
Now Red Fox drives slowly.

_____
- -
_____

Brainwork! Write a title for each story.

Read the story.

"Take off your coat," said the wind.
"I will blow and blow."
The man did not take it off.
"Take off your coat," said the sun.
"I will shine and shine."
The man did take off his coat!

Write the answer to each question.

1. Who can shine?

_____

_____

2. Who can blow?

_____

_____

3. Who is walking?

_____

_____

4. What is the man wearing?

_____

_____

5. Why does the man take off the coat?

_____

_____

Read the story.

"I want the grapes," said the fox.
So he jumped up to get them.
He missed.
He jumped again and again.
He missed again and again.
He did not get the grapes.
"They are not good anyway,"
said the fox. And he left.

Circle the correct answers.

1. The | dog | fox | wants something.

2. The fox | jumps | runs | to get the grapes.

3. The fox wants | cake | grapes | .

4. He | gets | misses | the grapes.

5. The fox says the grapes are | good | not good | .

6. The fox jumps | one time | many times | .

7. The grapes are | up high | down low | .

Homework Helper Record

Color the bean for each page you complete.

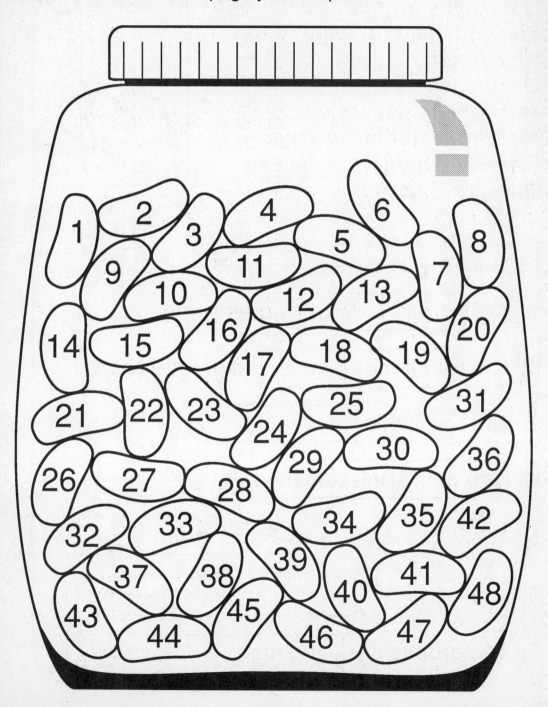

FS-8136 Homework Helpers—Reading 1

HOMEWORK AWARD

presented to

_____

for successfully completing
this Homework Helper Book

_____
signed

_____
date